Power Maths

Year 1
Textbook 1C

Series Editor: Tony Staneff

White Rose Maths Edition

Astrid

Astrid is brave.

She likes to help if you get stuck.

helpful

flexible

curious

determined

Sparks

Flo

Ash

Dexter

Series editor: Tony Staneff
Lead author: Josh Lury
Consultants (first edition): Professor Liu Jian and Professor Zhang Dan
Author team (first edition): Tony Staneff, Josh Lury, Kelsey Brown, Jenny Lewis, Beth Smith, Paul Wrangles, Liu Jian, Zhou Da, Zhang Dan, Yan Lili and Wang Mingming

Pearson

Contents

This shows us what page to turn to.

I wonder what new things we will find!

How to use this book

Do you remember how to use Power Maths?

These pages help us get ready for a new unit. →

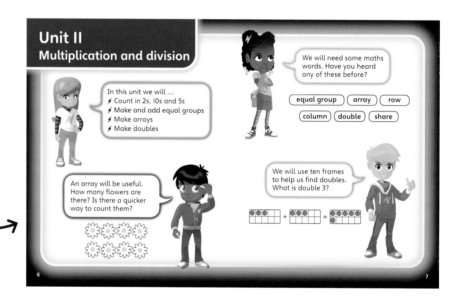

Discover

Lessons start with Discover.

Have fun exploring new maths problems.

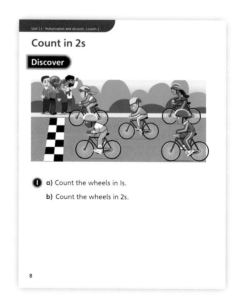

Share

Next, we share what we found out.

Did we all solve the problems the same way?

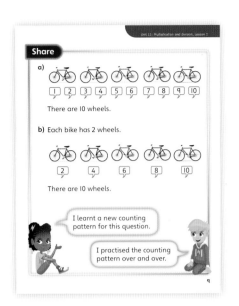

Think together

Then we have a go at some more problems together.

We will try a challenge too!

This tells you which page to go to in your Practice Book.

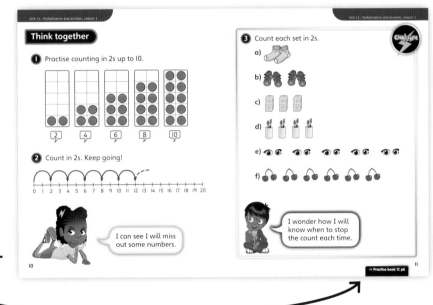

At the end of a unit we will show how much we can do!

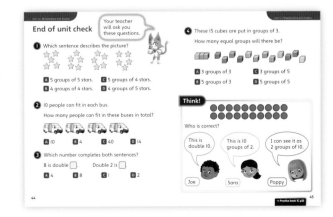

Unit II
Multiplication and division

In this unit we will ...
- Count in 2s, 10s and 5s
- Make and add equal groups
- Make arrays
- Make doubles

An array will be useful. How many flowers are there? Is there a quicker way to count them?

We will need some maths words. Have you heard any of these before?

equal group   array   row

column   double   share

We will use ten frames to help us find doubles. What is double 3?

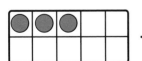 + 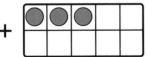 =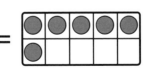

Count in 2s

Discover

1 **a)** Count the wheels in 1s.

b) Count the wheels in 2s.

Share

a)

| 1 | 2 | 3 | 4 | 5 | 6 | 7 | 8 | 9 | 10 |

There are 10 wheels.

b) Each bike has 2 wheels.

| 2 | 4 | 6 | 8 | 10 |

There are 10 wheels.

I learnt a new counting pattern for this question.

I practised the counting pattern over and over.

Think together

1 Practise counting in 2s up to 10.

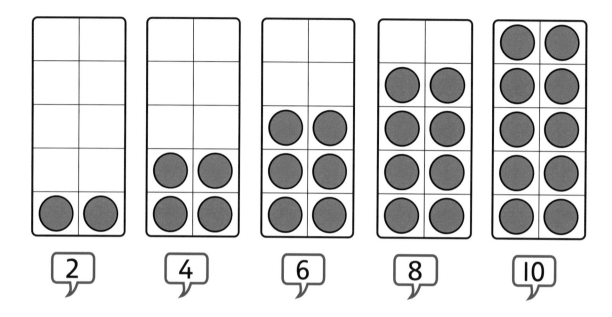

2 Count in 2s. Keep going!

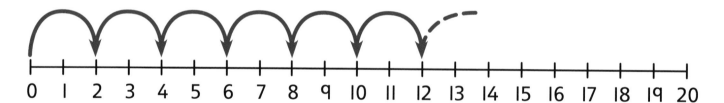

I can see I will miss out some numbers.

3 Count each set in 2s.

a)

b)

c)

d)

e)

f)

I wonder how I will know when to stop the count each time.

11

→ Practice book 1C p6

Count in 10s

Discover

1 **a)** Show 10 on your fingers or with cubes.

   b) Show 10 to a partner. They should do the same.

   What number did you both make altogether?

Share

a) You can show 10 like this.

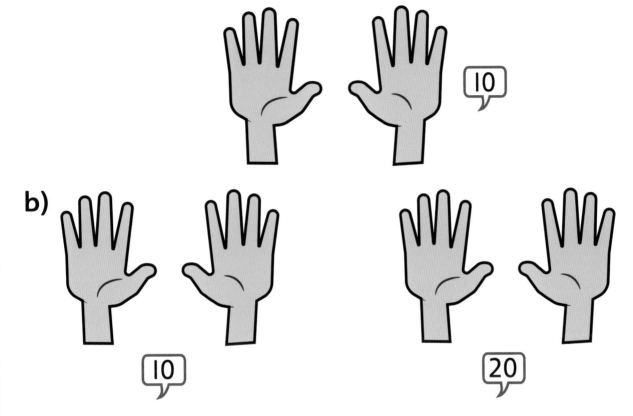

b)

2 tens is 20 altogether.

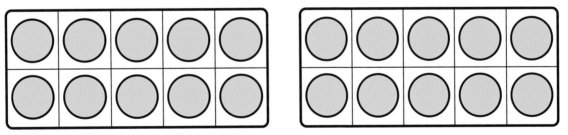

I made 2 tens using ten frames.

Think together

1 Count in 10s.

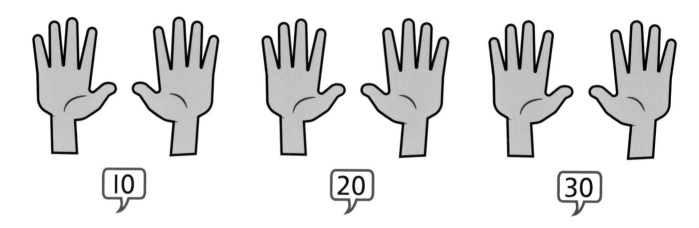

10   20   30

2 Count in 10s.

3 **a)** Point and count in 10s.

1	2	3	4	5	6	7	8	9	⑩
11	12	13	14	15	16	17	18	19	⑳
21	22	23	24	25	26	27	28	29	㉚
31	32	33	34	35	36	37	38	39	㊵
41	42	43	44	45	46	47	48	49	㊿

b) Point and count in 10s.

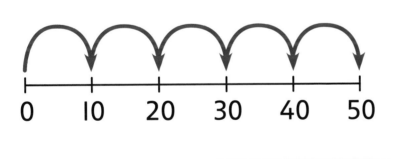

0   10   20   30   40   50

I wonder if thirTEEN is the same as thirTY.

→ Practice book 1C p9

Count in 5s

Discover

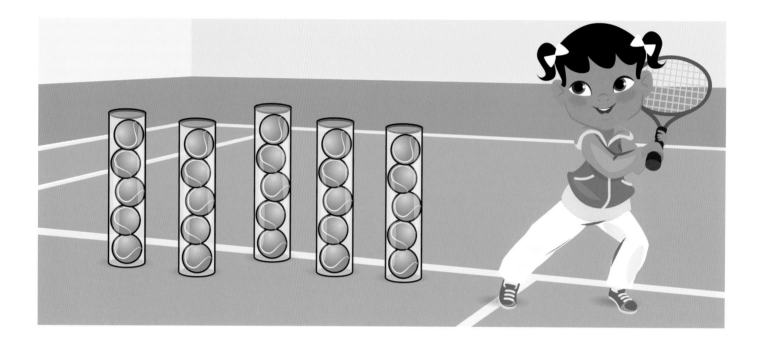

1 **a)** How many balls are there in each tube?

   b) Count the total number of tennis balls in the tubes.

Share

a) Each tube has 5 tennis balls.

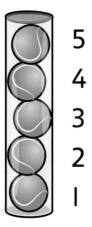

5
4
3
2
1

I checked
each tube.

b)

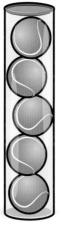  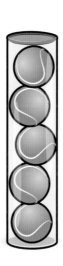 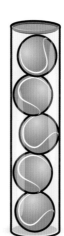 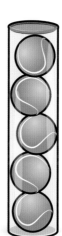

5   10   15   20   25

There are 25 tennis balls in total.

I used a number
line to help me.

Think together

1 Practise this new counting pattern.

5   10   15   20   25   30   35   40   45   50

I can hear a rhythm as I count in 5s.

2 Count in 5s.

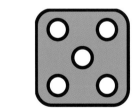  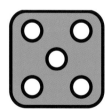 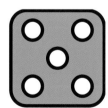

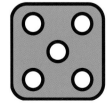 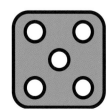 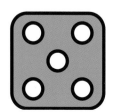 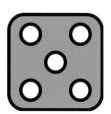

3 **a)** Point and count in 5s.

Cover all the numbers you say with cubes.

1	2	3	4	5	6	7	8	9	10
11	12	13	14	15	16	17	18	19	20
21	22	23	24	25	26	27	28	29	30
31	32	33	34	35	36	37	38	39	40
41	42	43	44	45	46	47	48	49	50

b) Point and count in 5s.

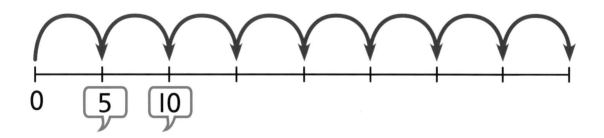

19

Equal groups

Discover

1 **a)** How many rowing boats are there?

How many people are there

in each rowing boat?

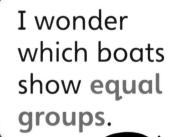

I wonder which boats show **equal groups**.

b) How many sailing boats are there?

Are there the same number of

people in each sailing boat?

Share

a)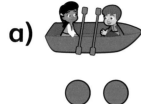

2   2   2   2

There are 4 rowing boats.

There are 4 groups. They are equal groups.

There are 2 people in each rowing boat.

There are 4 groups of 2 people.

b)

 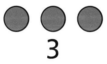 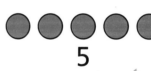

1   3   5

There are 3 sailing boats.

One sailing boat has 1 person in it.

One sailing boat has 3 people in it.

One sailing boat has 5 people in it.

The rowing boats show equal groups.

The sailing boats do not show equal groups.

Think together

1 How many glasses are there?

How many ice cubes are added to each glass?

There are ☐ groups of ☐ ice cubes.

2 Use cubes or counters to make 3 equal groups.

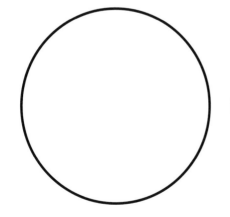 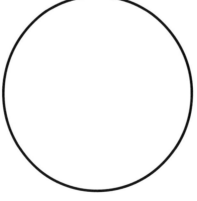 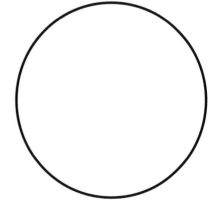

3 equal groups of ☐.

3 Which shows equal groups?

CHALLENGE

A

B

C

If they are not equal groups, I wonder how to make them into equal groups.

23

→ Practice book 1C p15

Add equal groups

Discover

1 **a)** Count the shoes.

b) Count the flowers.

Share

a) The shoes are in groups of 2. Count in 2s.

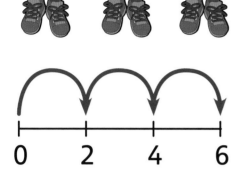

I remembered the counting pattern we learnt in another lesson.

There are 6 shoes.

$2 + 2 + 2 = 6$

b) The flowers are in groups of 5. Count in 5s.

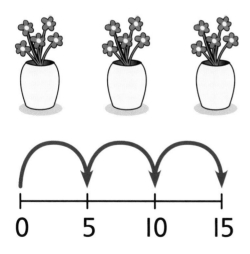

There are 15 flowers.

$5 + 5 + 5 = 15$

Think together

1 Count in 10s.

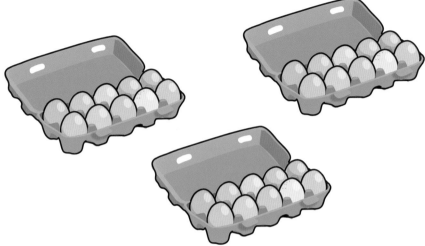

10 + 10 + 10 = ☐

2 Count the scores.

a) Kat's score

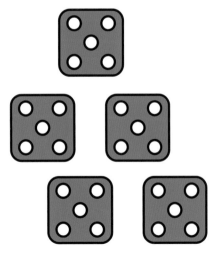

b) Ben's score

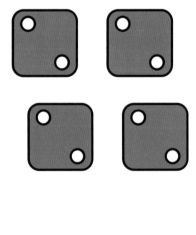

3 Match each picture to the correct calculation.

CHALLENGE

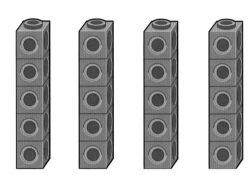

$2 + 2 + 2$

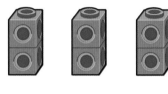

$5 + 5 + 5 + 5$

$5 + 5 + 5$

$10 + 10$

→ Practice book 1C p18

Make arrays

Discover

1 **a)** How many seeds are there in each **row**?

How many rows are there?

How many seeds are there in total?

b) Make 2 rows of 10 from counters or cubes.

Share

a)

There are 10 seeds in each row.

There are 2 rows.

10 + 10 = 20

There are 20 seeds in total.

b)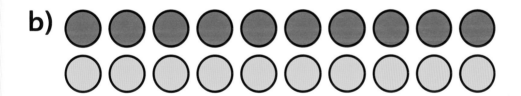

I used different coloured counters to show each row.

Think together

1 **a)** Copy the **array**.

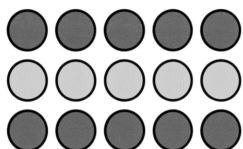

I will copy the array using cubes

b) Complete the sentence.

There are ☐ rows of ☐.

c) Count equal groups to find the total for the array.

2 Count the equal groups to find the total in each array.

a)

b)

3 **a)** Copy the arrays.

Count the equal groups to find each total.

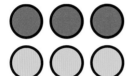 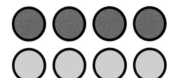 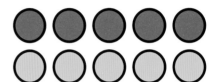

You can see rows and **columns** in arrays.

b) Explain to your partner why this is not an array.

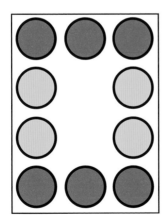

→ Practice book 1C p21

Make doubles

Discover

If you roll 2 dice with the same number, it is called a double.

1 **a)** Who rolled a **double**?

b) Work out double 4.

Share

a) Tariq rolled 4 and 4.

That is double 4.

Tariq rolled a double.

Mia rolled 2 and 3.

That is not a double.

b) Double 4 is 8.

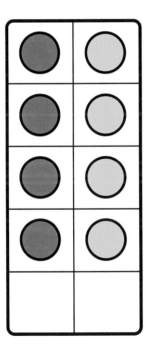

You can show doubles on your fingers.

Think together

1 Work out each double.

a)

Double 2 is ☐.

b)

Double 3 is ☐.

2 Work out each double up to double 5.

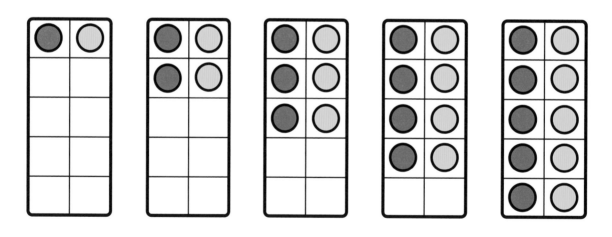

3 Place more counters to work out doubles up to double 10.

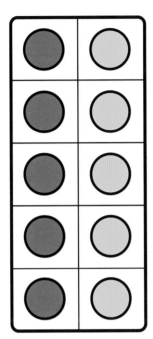

I am going to learn my doubles.

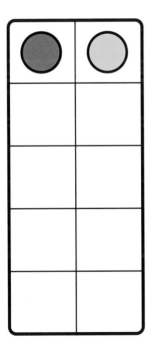

→ Practice book 1C p24

Grouping

Discover

1 **a)** How many children are there?
What groups are they in?

Show the groups and the total using counters or cubes.

b) Put the children in groups of 2.

Show the groups using counters or cubes.

Share

a) 1 group of 2

1 group of 3

1 group of 5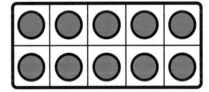

There are 10 children in total.

b)

5 equal groups of 2.

Think together

1 Here are 12 children.

They need to sit in groups of 4.

How many groups of children will there be?

> I will use 12 counters and put them into groups of 4.

2

There are 12 socks.

The socks are put into groups of 2.

How many groups are there?

3 Use 20 multilink cubes.

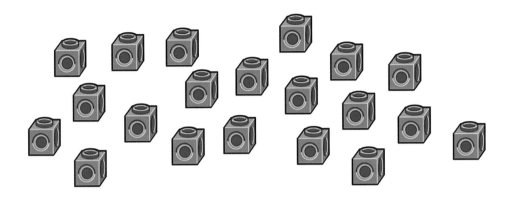

a) Make towers 5 cubes tall.
How many towers of the same height can you make?

b) Make towers 10 cubes tall.
How many towers of the same height can you make?

c) Make towers 4 cubes tall.
How many towers of the same height can you make?

d) Make towers 2 cubes tall.
How many towers of the same height can you make?

e) What happens when you try to make towers 3 cubes tall?

→ Practice book 1C p27

Sharing

Discover

Let's share fairly ...

1 **a)** **Share** 10 strawberries between 2 children.

b) Practise sharing 10 counters between 2.

Share

a) There are 10 strawberries altogether.

One for you, ... one for me, ... one for you, ... one for me.

10 shared between 2 is 5 each.

b)

10 shared between 2 is always 5 each.

Think together

1 Share 6 between 2.

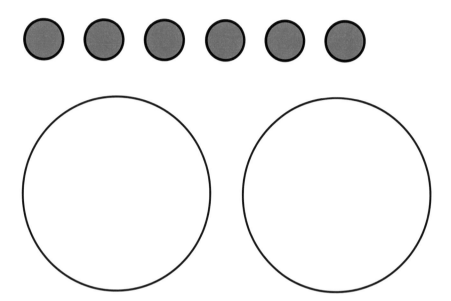

2 Share 6 between 3.

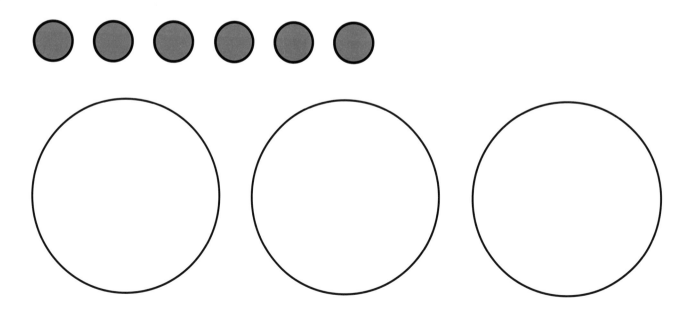

3

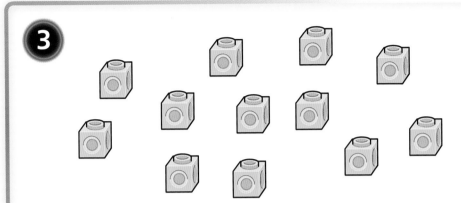

a) Share the cubes between 2 children.

How many cubes will they each get?

b) Share the cubes between 3 children.

How many cubes will they each get?

c) Share the cubes between 4 children.

How many cubes will they each get?

d) Share the cubes between 5 children.

How many cubes will they each get?

e) What do you notice?

→ Practice book 1C p30

End of unit check

Your teacher will ask you these questions.

1 Which sentence describes the picture?

A 5 groups of 5 stars.   **C** 5 groups of 4 stars.

B 4 groups of 4 stars.   **D** 4 groups of 5 stars.

2 10 people can fit in each bus.

How many people can fit in these buses in total?

A 10   **B** 4   **C** 40   **D** 14

3 Which number completes both sentences?

8 is double ☐.   Double 2 is ☐.

A 4   **B** 8   **C** 1   **D** 2

4 These 15 cubes are put in groups of 3.

How many equal groups will there be?

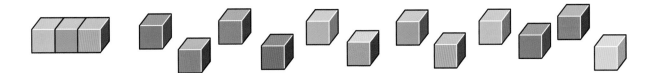

A 3 groups of 3   **C** 3 groups of 5

B 5 groups of 3   **D** 5 groups of 5

Think!

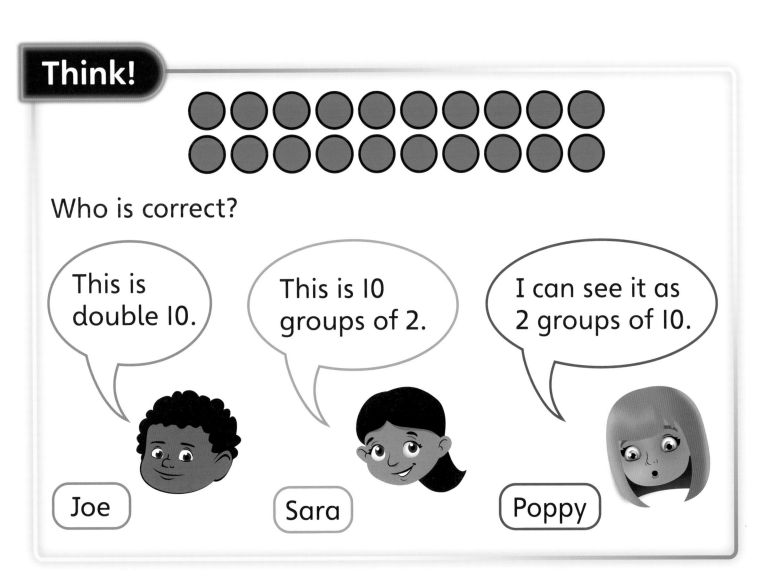

Who is correct?

Joe: This is double 10.

Sara: This is 10 groups of 2.

Poppy: I can see it as 2 groups of 10.

45

→ Practice book 1C p33

Unit 12
Fractions

In this unit we will …
- ⚡ Find half of a shape or a quantity
- ⚡ Share equally
- ⚡ Find a quarter of a shape or a quantity

We can find half of a shape. Which shape has been cut in half?

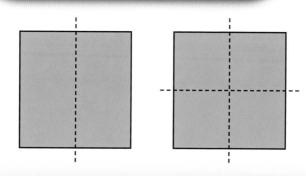

We will be using these maths words. Can you read them out loud?

(half)   (halves)   (quarter)

(whole)   (part)

We will also do some sharing. Share the jam tarts equally. How many does each child get?

Recognise and find a half of a shape

Discover

1 **a)** Fold a sheet of paper in **half**.

   b) Shade in one half of your piece of paper.

Share

a)

When you split a **whole** into two equal parts, each **part** is a half.

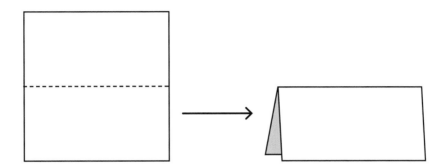

b) There are different ways to shade one half.

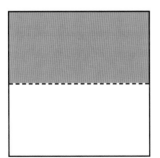

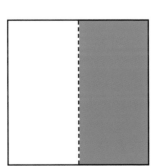

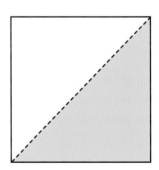

Think together

1 Which shape is half shaded?

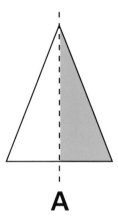

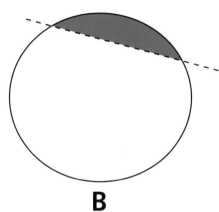

A

B

2 Copy each shape. Split each shape into **halves**. Shade one half of each shape.

a)

c)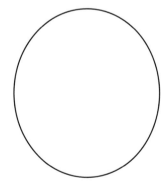

b)

d)

③

CHALLENGE

The gardeners have a piece of string.

How can they split the string into two halves?

I wonder how I can find half-way along a line.

51

→ Practice book 1C p35

Recognise and find a half of a quantity

Discover

1 **a)** Share the apples equally between two horses.

b) Show how to find half of 8 apples.

Share

a) There are 8 apples in total.

One for him, one for her, one for him, one for her, …

8 shared equally between 2 is 4.

b)

The whole is 8.
One half is 4.

4 is half of 8.

Think together

1 Share 6 carrots between 2 donkeys.

Half of 6 is ☐.

2 Which groups of apples have been shared into halves?

A

C
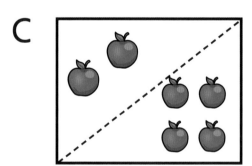

B
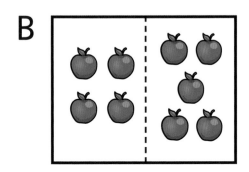

D
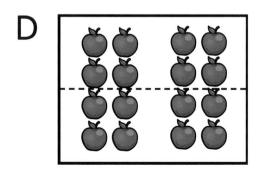

3 Tim and Meg are making doubles and halves.

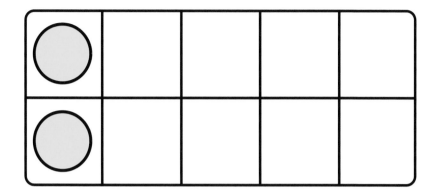

Double 1 is 2.

Half of 2 is 1.

Make your own doubles and halves.

→ Practice book 1C p38

Recognise and find a quarter of a shape

Discover

1 **a)** Describe the parts of the board.

b) Split a square into **quarters** in another way.

Share

a)

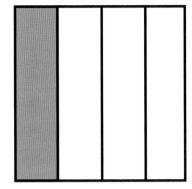

When you split a **whole** into 4 equal parts, each **part** is a **quarter**.

There are 4 equal parts.
Each part is one quarter.

b) Here are other ways to split a square into quarters.

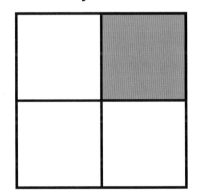 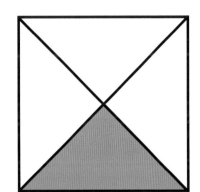

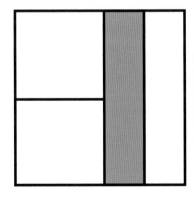

Is the last shape split into quarters? The parts don't look the same.

There are 4 equal parts.
Each part is 1 quarter.

Think together

1 Which boards are split into equal parts?
Which board is split into quarters?

A   B   C

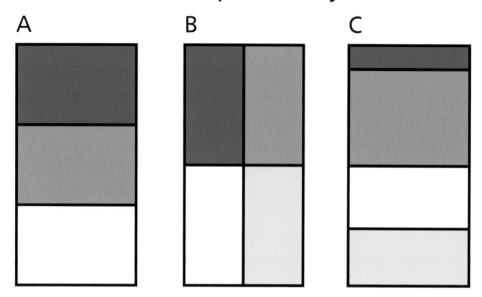

2 Mia says she has divided her circle into quarters.
Do you agree?

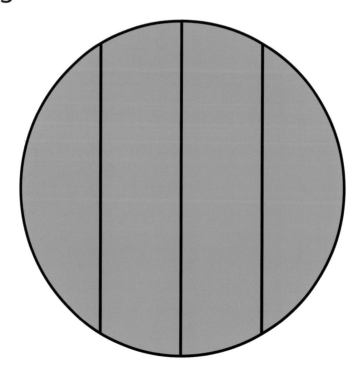

58

3 Fold a strip of paper in half, then in half again.

What will happen when you open it up?

I think it will have 2 parts because I did 2 folds.

I think I fold makes halves, so 2 folds will make more parts.

→ Practice book 1C p41

Recognise and find a quarter of a quantity

Discover

I **a)** The children share the oranges equally.

How many does each child get?

b) This is a quarter of another tray of oranges.

What is the whole?

Share

a)

To share
between 4,
I split them
into quarters.

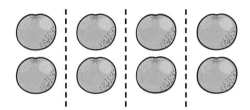

I shared the
oranges out
one by one.

Each child gets 2 oranges.

b)

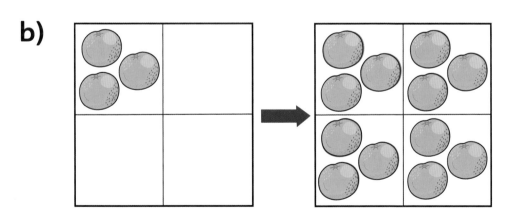

There are 3 oranges in each quarter.

The whole is 12 oranges.

Think together

1 Find one quarter of 4.

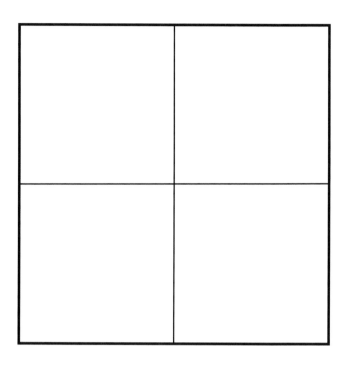

2 One quarter is 4 pears. What is the whole?

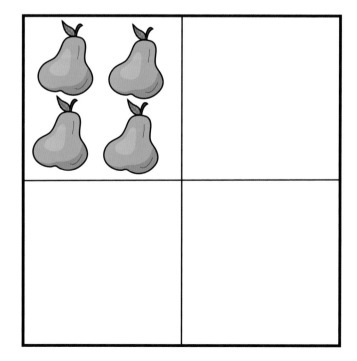

3 **a)** Count the total number of counters.

What is one quarter of the total number of counters?

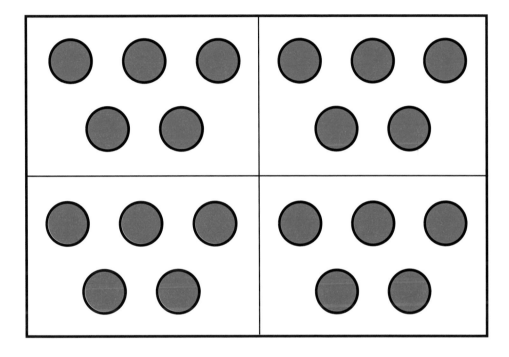

b) Work out one quarter of 24.

I will use some counters and share between 4 boxes.

→ **Practice book 1C p44**

End of unit check

Your teacher will ask you these questions.

1 Which pizza is cut into halves?

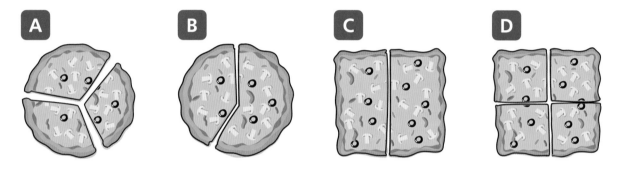

A   B   C   D

2 There are 12 frogs. Half are male.

How many are male?

A 10   B 6   C 2   D 12

3 Which window is not split into quarters?

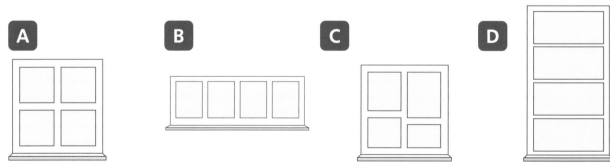

A   B   C   D

4 Which number completes both sentences?

2 is half of ☐.

☐ is a quarter of 16.

A 1   **B** 8   **C** 2   **D** 4

Think!

Luke says, 'I would like half of them.'

Eva says, 'I would like a quarter, please.'

Luke works out half, but Eva is stuck.

Can you explain why?

These words will help you.

half   quarter

whole   part

split

65

→ Practice book 1C p47

Unit 13
Position and direction

In this unit we will …
⚡ Describe turns
⚡ Use the words left and right
⚡ Say if something is above or below something else
⚡ Say if something is moving forwards or backwards

We will use these arrows to show turns. Which one do you think shows a whole turn?

 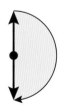 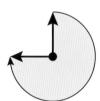 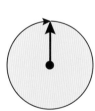

These maths words help us talk about where something is. Do you know any of these?

turn | half turn | quarter turn | whole turn
left | right | forwards | backwards
above | below | top | middle | bottom
first | second | third | fourth

Look at where these animals are. Which animal is on the bottom shelf?

Describe turns

Discover

1 **a)** Tom is pointing at the rock. He does a
   half turn.

   What will he point to now?

   b) Try different half turns with Tom facing a
   different object each time.

   What do you notice?

Share

For a half turn, it is the same no matter which way you turn.

a)

Tom will point to the tree.

b)

These are all half turns.

I can see that when I make a half turn, I will turn to look in exactly the opposite direction.

Think together

1 Here are some different **quarter turns**.

Do some quarter turns in different directions.
Do you end up facing a different direction if you
change the way you turn?

2 Tom makes a quarter turn.
What will he be facing?

Dont forget,
quarter turns can
be in different
directions.

70

CHALLENGE

3 Put different objects in the boxes. Use a toy to practise half, quarter and whole turns.

I wonder what happens if I try 2 quarter turns.

I will try 3 quarter turns. Or even 4.

71

Describe position – left and right

Discover

1 **a)** What is on the **left** side of the road?

b) What is on the **right** side of the road?

Share

a)

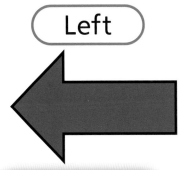

Left

This arrow is pointing left.

The cat is on the left of the road.
The tree is on the left of the road.

b)

Right

This arrow is pointing right.

The person is on the right of the road.
The house is on the right of the road.

Think together

1 Look **left**.

Look **right**.

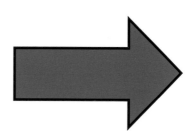

What can you see?

2 Lift your left hand.

Lift your right hand.

Point to your left foot.

Point to your right foot.

3 Talk about this line of animals.

CHALLENGE

a) Which animal is on the left?

b) Which animal is on the right?

c) Which animal is in the middle?

d) Which animal is on the left of the zebra?

e) Which animal is on the right of the lion?

I will make up my own questions for my partner to check they know their left and right.

75

→ Practice book 1C p52

Describe position – forwards and backwards

Discover

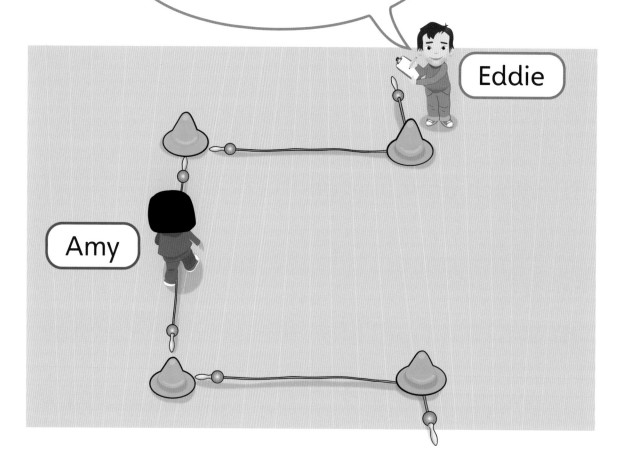

I a) When Amy gets to the next cone, what turn will she make?

Will she turn left or right?

b) When Amy has turned the corner, what does Eddie need to say to help her get to the end of the maze?

Share

a) Amy will make a quarter turn right.

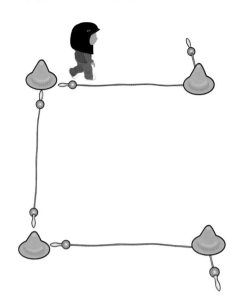

b) Walk **forwards**.

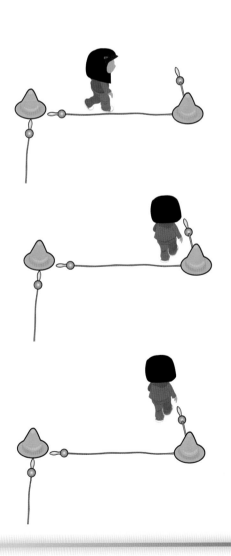

Make a quarter turn left.

Walk forwards.

Think together

1 Describe the route Amy takes here. The first part is already done for you.

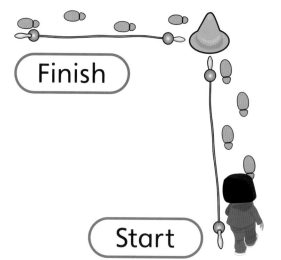

1. Walk forwards 4 steps.

2. _____

3. _____

2 Describe Amy's route from start to finish. The first part is already done for you.

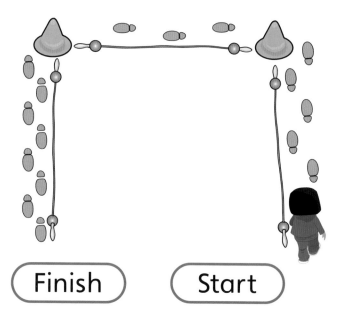

1. Walk forwards 5 steps.

2. _____

3. _____

4. _____

5. _____

3

CHALLENGE

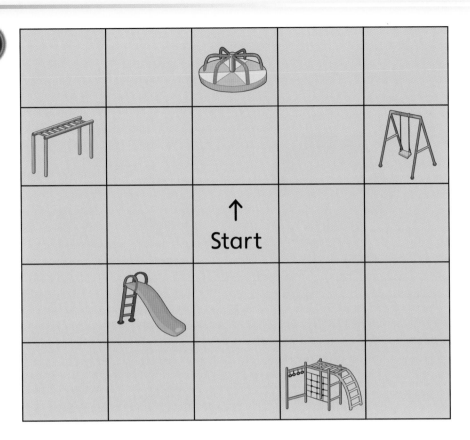

Begin at Start and follow the instructions.

1. Walk 1 square forwards.

2. Make a quarter turn left.

3. Walk 2 squares forwards.

Where do you end up?

I will make up a story to get to a different place in the playground.

I wonder what happens if you say 'Walk 2 squares **backwards**' for number 3.

79

Describe position – above and below

1 **a)** What is **above** the dinosaur?

b) Describe the **position** of the teddy.

Share

a)

The books are above the dinosaur.

b)

top

middle

bottom

The teddy is on the bottom shelf.

The teddy is **below** the rings.

I described the position differently.
The teddy is on the right of the robot.

Think together

1 Look at the shelves

a) Which shelf is the teddy on?

b) Point to the object above the teddy.

c) What objects are on the top shelf?

2 Here is a grid.

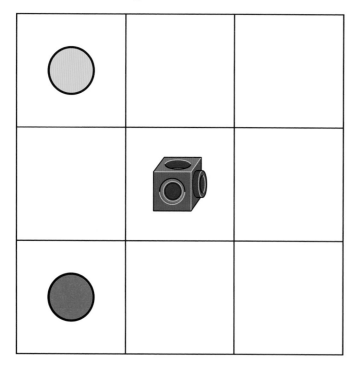

Put another counter in the bottom row.
Ask a partner to describe its position.

3 Here are some objects.

Pick an object. Don't show your partner.

a) Tell your partner what is above or below your object.

Can they work out which is your object?

b) Your partner should pick a different object. They must tell you what is left or right of it.

Can you work out which is their object?

→ Practice book 1C p58

Ordinal numbers

Discover

1 **a)** What is the **second** activity?

b) What is the **fourth** activity?

Share

The children have to do 4 activities.

| first | second | third | fourth |
| 1st | 2nd | 3rd | 4th |

a) The second activity is throwing a bean bag into a bucket.

b) The fourth activity is jumping over some buckets.

Think together

1 Point to the people and say who is first, second, third, fourth and fifth.

2 What is on the fourth pizza?

chicken   peppers   cheese   meat   mushroom   olives

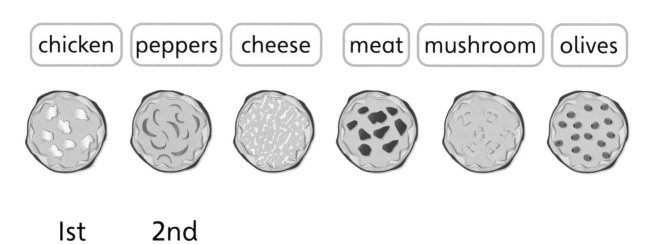

1st   2nd

3 Who comes after the sixth person?

Asha Meg Milo Joe Ola Tim Jack Lou

1st   2nd

I think it is Tim.

I think it is more than one person.

87

→ Practice book 1C p61

End of unit check

Your teacher will ask you these questions.

1 Which sentence **does not** describe the image?

A The horse is to the left of the sheep.

B The sheep is in between the horse and the duck.

C The duck is to the right of the sheep.

D The sheep is to the left of the horse.

2 Complete the sentence.

The pear is _____ the orange.

A above   C to the right of

B below   D to the left of

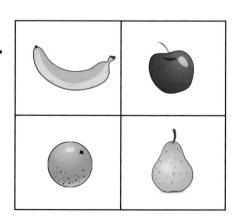

3 Tom is facing the swing.

He turns a quarter turn to his left.

What is he facing now?

A house   **C** swing

B car   **D** bike

Think!

Guide the mouse to the cheese.

Find more than one path.

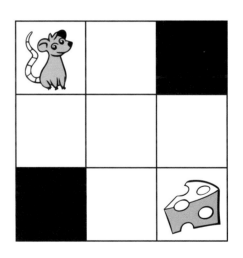

These words might help you.

forwards   backwards

left   right

half turn   quarter turn

→ Practice book 1C p64

Unit 14
Numbers to 100

In this unit we will ...
- ⚡ Count in 10s
- ⚡ Learn how to use a 100 square
- ⚡ Use 10s and 1s to make larger numbers
- ⚡ Say which number is larger and smaller

We will use this 100 square. Can you find the number 30?

1	2	3	4	5	6	7	8	9	10
11	12	13	14	15	16	17	18	19	20
21	22	23	24	25	26	27	28	29	30
31	32	33	34	35	36	37	38	39	40
41	42	43	44	45	46	47	48	49	50
51	52	53	54	55	56	57	58	59	60
61	62	63	64	65	66	67	68	69	70
71	72	73	74	75	76	77	78	79	80
81	82	83	84	85	86	87	88	89	90
91	92	93	94	95	96	97	98	99	100

We will need some maths words.
Can you read these out loud?

100 square

one more

one less

greater than

less than

tens (10s)

ones (1s)

We will need these too.
What number is shown here?

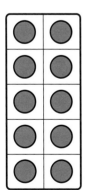 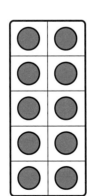 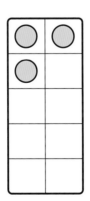

Count from 50 to 100

Discover

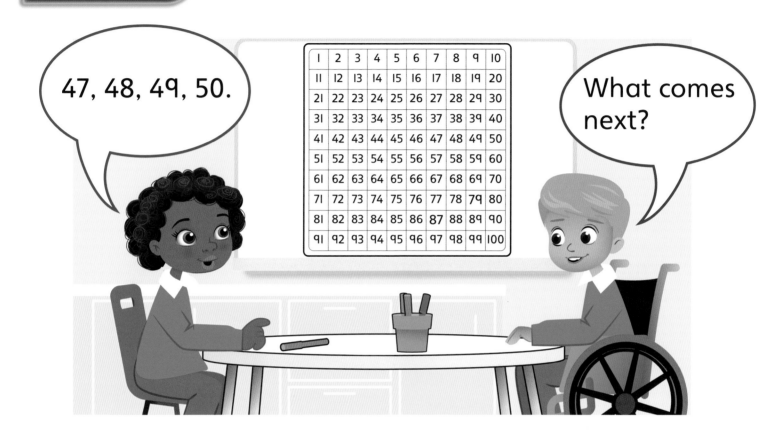

1 **a)** How do you count on a **100 square**?

Practise counting up to 100.

b) Play a game with a partner.

Cover a number.

Ask your partner to say the hidden number.

Share

a) and **b)**

I counted along each row then went back to start the next row.

1	2	3	4	5	6	7	8	9	10
11	12	13	14	15	16	17	18	19	20
21	22	23	24	25	26	27	28	29	30
31	32	33	34	35	36	37	38	39	40
41	42	43	44	45	46	47	48	49	50
51	52	53	54	55	56	57	58	59	60
61	62	63	64	65	66	67	68	69	70
71	72	73	74	✹	76	77	78	79	80
81	82	83	84	85	86	87	88	89	90
91	92	93	94	95	96	97	98	99	100

75 is covered here.

The numbers make lots of patterns. I will try and find some of them.

Think together

1 **a)** Point and count from 5I to 60.

5I	52	53	54	55	56	57	58	59	60

b) Point and count from 6I to 70.

6I	62	63	64	65	66	67	68	69	70

2 What numbers are hidden?

I	2	3	4	5	6	7	8		10
II	12	13	14	15	16	17	18	19	20
21	22	23	24	25	26	27	28	29	30
	32	33	34	35	36	37	38	39	40
41	42	43	44	45	46	47	48	49	50
5I	52	53	54	55	56	57	58		60
6I	62	63	64	65	66	67	68	69	70
	72	73	74	75	76	77	78		80
	82	83	84	85	86	87	88	89	90
9I	92	93	94	95	96	97	98		100

3 Play a game.
Each player can use a different colour counter.

Start on 0.
Move I, 2 or 3 spaces.
Say the numbers you land on as you jump.
Take turns. Keep going until you get to 100.

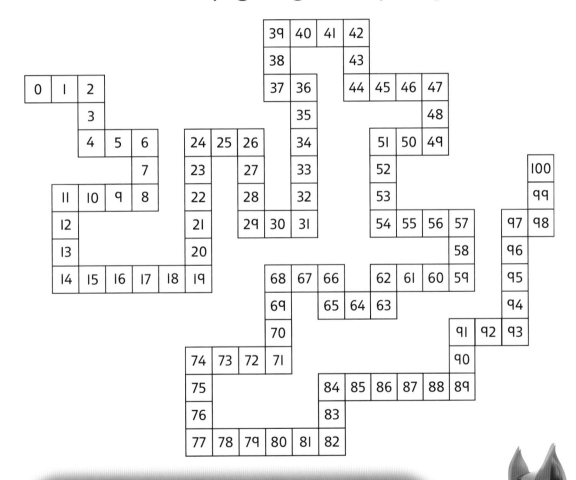

You can also play the game counting back from 100 to 0.

95

→ Practice book 1C p66

10s to 100

Discover

1 **a)** What numbers are covered?

b) Show 10 on your fingers.

Count in 10s as a class.

Share

a)

1	2	3	4	5	6	7	8	9	**10**
11	12	13	14	15	16	17	18	19	**20**
21	22	23	24	25	26	27	28	29	**30**
31	32	33	34	35	36	37	38	39	**40**
41	42	43	44	45	46	47	48	49	**50**
51	52	53	54	55	56	57	58	59	**60**
61	62	63	64	65	66	67	68	69	**70**
71	72	73	74	75	76	77	78	79	**80**
81	82	83	84	85	86	87	88	89	**90**
91	92	93	94	95	96	97	98	99	**100**

All of the 10s were covered.

b)

10

You can count in 10s using your fingers.
This is 5 tens.

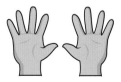 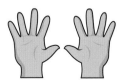 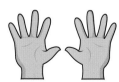 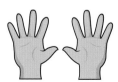 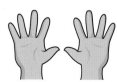

10   20   30   40   50

Think together

1 What number are the children showing?

 I will count in 1s.

I will count in 10s.

2 Count the 10s.

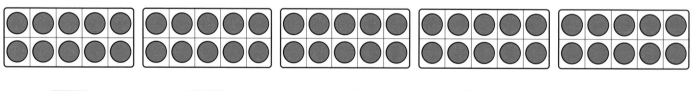

 10   20   30

3 **a)** There are 10 flowers in each bunch.

How many flowers are there altogether?

b) There are 10 sweets in each bag.

How many sweets are there altogether?

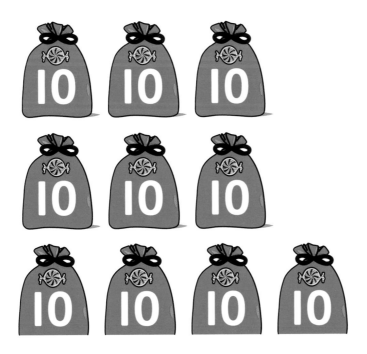

→ **Practice book 1C p69**

Partition into 10s and 1s

Discover

Days of ☀

1 **a)** How many days of sun have there been?
Count in 1s.

b) How many days of sun have there been?
This time count the 10s and then the 1s.

Share

a) There have been 31 days of sun.

I counted in 1s.

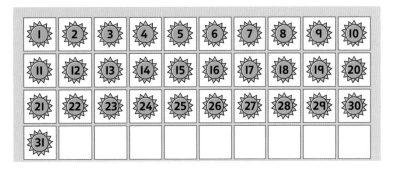

b)

I counted in 10s and then counted 1 more.

Think together

1 Count the number of rainy days.

Days of 💧

2 Count the 10s then the extra 1s.

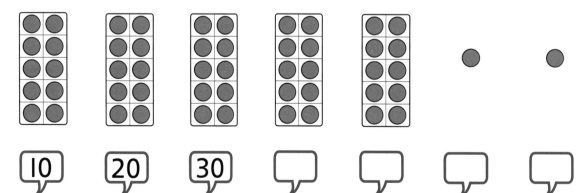

10   20   30

3 Zak has circled 10s.

CHALLENGE

a) How many 10s are there?
How many extra 1s are there?

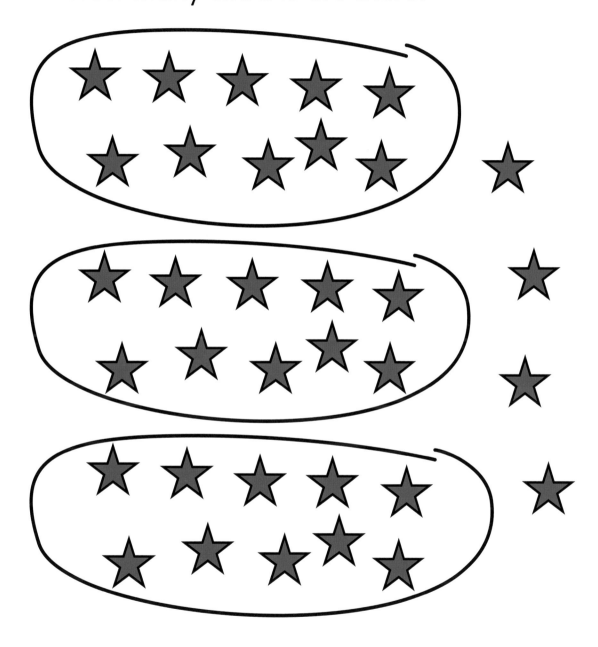

b) How many stars are there altogether?

→ **Practice book 1C p72**

Number line to 100

Discover

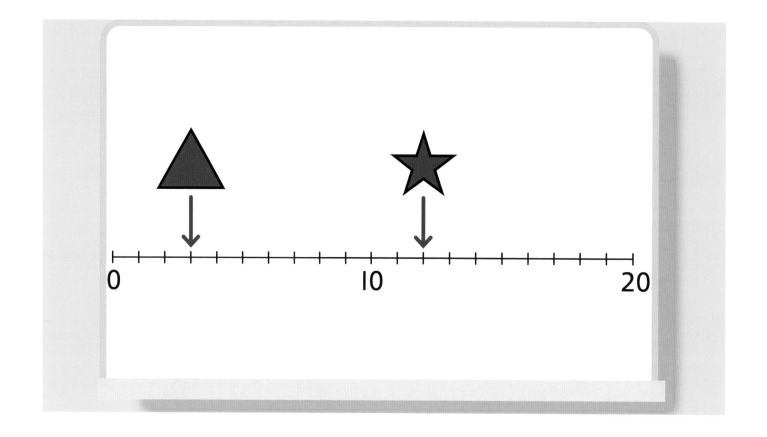

1 **a)** What number is marked by the triangle?

What number is marked by the star?

b) What number comes next after 20?

Share

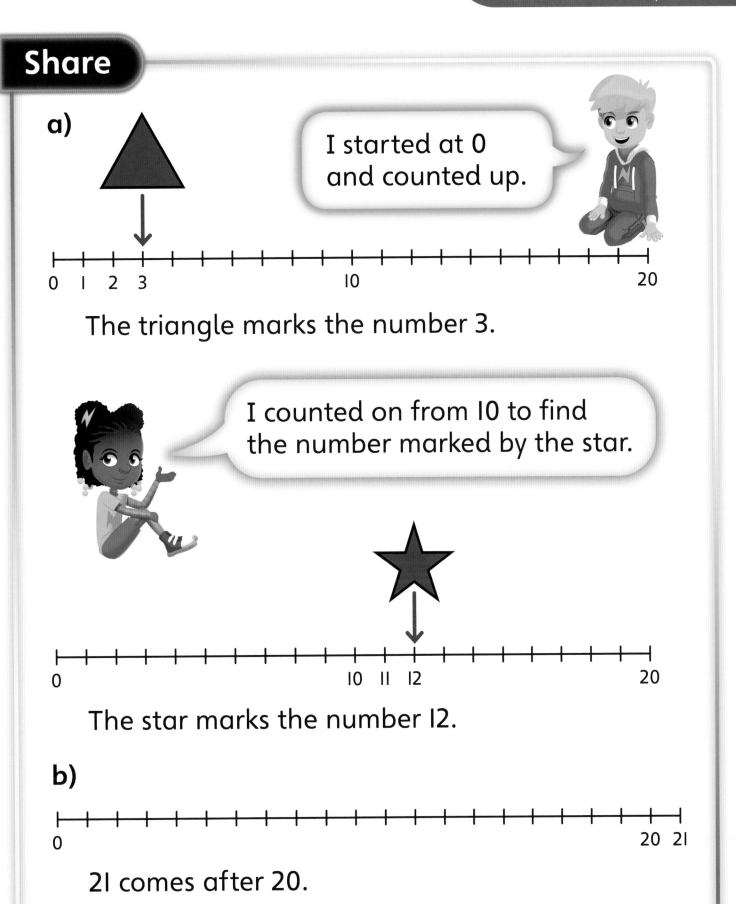

a)

I started at 0 and counted up.

The triangle marks the number 3.

I counted on from 10 to find the number marked by the star.

The star marks the number 12.

b)

21 comes after 20.

Think together

1 Point to 21 and 29 on this number line.

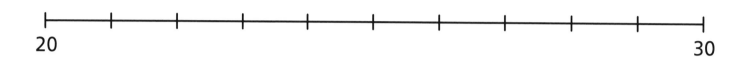

20   30

2 What are the missing numbers on these number lines?

a)

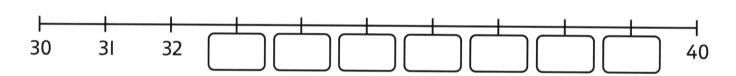

30   31   32   40

b)

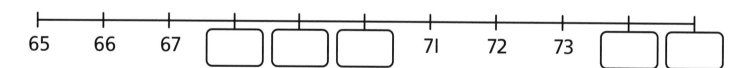

65   66   67   71   72   73

c)

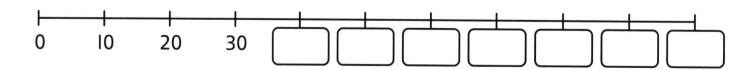

0   10   20   30

3 **a)** Point to where you think 45 should go on each number line.

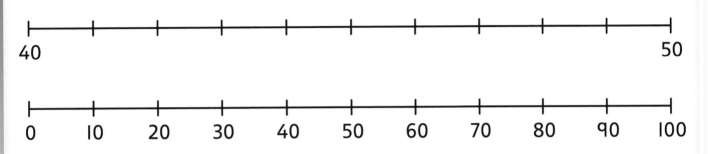

40   50

0   10   20   30   40   50   60   70   80   90   100

I know something about where 45 lies.

b) Point to where 93 should go.

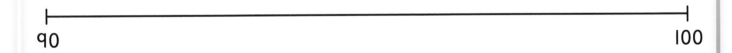

90   100

107

→ Practice book 1C p75

One more and one less

Discover

1 **a)** How many shells are there?

b) Rico finds one more shell.

How many shells are there now?

Share

a)

b)

One more than 35 is 36.

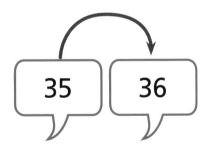

Think together

1 What is one more than each number?

a)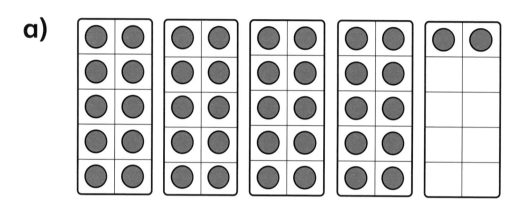

b)

2 Max has **84** flowers.

Max gives a friend one flower.

How many flowers does he have now?

He gives another friend one flower.

How many flowers does he have now?

3 Work out one more and one less than each number.

a)

57

b)

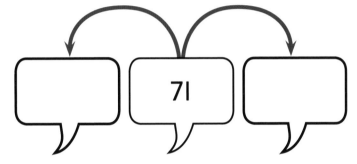

71

c)

50

I wonder what the missing numbers are in this diagram.

66

111

Compare numbers

Discover

I collected 39 leaves.

I collected 35 leaves.

Sunil

Seth

1 **a)** Make each number on ten frames or using cubes.

b) Who collected more leaves?

Share

a) Sunil collected 35 leaves.

Seth collected 39 leaves.

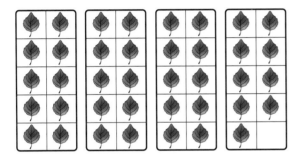

b) Seth collected more leaves.

				Sunil				Seth	
31	32	33	34	35	36	37	38	39	40

I used a number track to work out which number is greater.

I saw that Seth had collected more.

Think together

1 Which number is smaller?

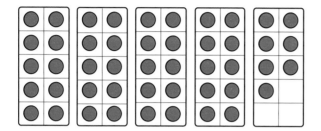

41	42	43	44	45	46	47	48	49	50

2 Choose a number greater than 65.

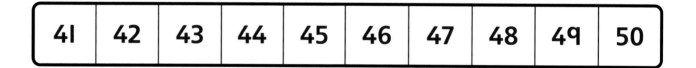

I can find different answers to this question.

3 **a)** Compare the numbers 38 and 29.
Which number is greater?

A 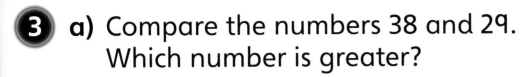 B

> I think I can compare the numbers by just looking at the 10s.

b) How can you use the hundred square to compare 38 and 29?

1	2	3	4	5	6	7	8	9	10
11	12	13	14	15	16	17	18	19	20
21	22	23	24	25	26	27	28	29	30
31	32	33	34	35	36	37	38	39	40
41	42	43	44	45	46	47	48	49	50
51	52	53	54	55	56	57	58	59	60
61	62	63	64	65	66	67	68	69	70
71	72	73	74	75	76	77	78	79	80
81	82	83	84	85	86	87	88	89	90
91	92	93	94	95	96	97	98	99	100

29 ◯ 38

> Remember that < means less than and > means greater than.

115

End of unit check

Your teacher will ask you these questions.

1 What is the next number?

34   35   36   37   38   39

A 310   B 30   C 40   D 100

2 How many biscuits are there?

A 13   B 9   C 63   D 90

3 My number is made up of 5 tens and 7 ones.

What is my number?

A 75   B 57   C 12   D 50

4 What number is the arrow pointing to?

20   30

A 7   B 26   C 27   D 29

5 Which of these numbers has 7 tens?

A 70   B 7   C 67   D All of them

Think!

Complete the target number grid.

Target number of 75

Make it	Describe it	Break it apart	Draw it
	75 is made up of _____ _____	75	

I will try it with different target numbers.

These words might help you.

more   less

tens   ones

117

Unit 15
Money

In this unit we will ...
- ⚡ Learn about coins
- ⚡ Learn about notes
- ⚡ Count in 1s, 2s, 5s and 10s using coins

Here are some coins. Do you know which is the 5 pence coin?

Have you heard these money words before?

pound   pence

coins   notes   greater than (>)

less than (<)

Do you remember these signs? > < Complete this sentence using > or <.

Recognise coins

Discover

Before

After

1 **a)** Which **coins** are in the tray to start with?

b) Which coin has been removed from the tray?

Pence: 1 2 5 10 20 50

Share

The number on the coin tells us how much the coin is worth.

a) The coins in the tray to start with are:

 1 **pence** coin

 20 pence coin

 2 pence coin

 50 pence coin

 5 pence coin

 1 **pound** coin

 10 pence coin

 2 pound coin

b)

The has been removed from the tray.

Think together

1 **a)** Point to the 50 pence coin.

b) Point to the 1 pound coin.

c) Point to the 5 pence coin.

2

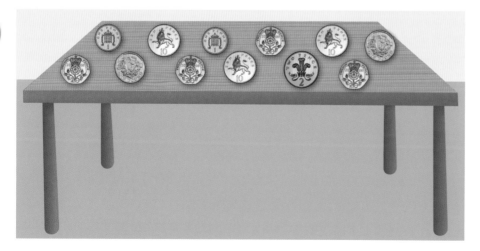

How many of each coin can you see?

Pence: 1 2 5 10 20 50

3

A 2 pence coin has the same value as two 1 pence coins.

 CHALLENGE

 is equal to   .

a) How many 1 pence coins are each of these coins worth?

b) Which coin has the greater value?

I think the 2 pence coin is worth more because it is bigger.

I am not sure that works for all the coins.

→ Practice book 1C p86

Recognise notes

Discover

1 **a)** What **notes** can you see?

b) Put the notes in order from least to greatest.

Pence: 1 2 5 10 20 50

Share

a) There are some:

The number on the note tells you what it is worth.

 5 pound notes

 10 pound notes

 20 pound notes

 50 pound notes

b)

least ⟶ greatest

Pounds: 1 2 5 10 20 50

Think together

I

Sponsorship money

Count the notes.

Copy and complete the table.

Note	How many?
£5	
£10	
£20	
£50	

Pence: I 2 5 10 20 50

2 Match the note to the correct words.

10 pounds

50 pounds

20 pounds

5 pounds

 3 Use < or > to complete the sentences.

a)

b)

c)

Pounds:  1 2 5 10   20   50 **127**

Count in coins

Discover

1 a) How much money is in each line?

b) Which line has the most coins?

Which line has the most money?

Pence: 1 2 5 10 20 50

Share

a)

I counted the coins.

There are five 1 pence coins.

> 1, 2, 3, 4, 5

There is 5 pence altogether.

There are four 2 pence coins.

> 2, 4, 6, 8

There is 8 pence altogether.

There are six 5 pence coins.

> 5, 10, 15, 20, 25, 30

There is 30 pence altogether.

There are four 10 pence coins.

> 10, 20, 30, 40

There is 40 pence altogether.

b) The most coins are in the 5 pence line.

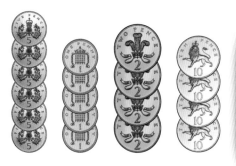

I noticed that the line with the most coins is not the line with the most money.

The most money is in the 10 pence line.

Think together

1 How much money is there in each row of coins?

a)

b)

c)

Pence: 1 2 5 10 20 50

2 Work out how much the coins in each group make. Then put >, < or = between them.

a)   ◯

b)

c)

3 Mia has 15 pence.

All her coins are the same.

Which of these coins could she have?

Explain your answer.

CHALLENGE

→ Practice book 1C p92

Pounds: 1 2 5 10 20 50

End of unit check

Your teacher will ask you these questions.

1 Which coin is worth 20 pence?

A    B   C    D

2 Which one is worth five pounds?

A   B   C    D

3 How much money is here altogether?

A 10 pence   B 2 pence   C 5 pence   D 8 pence

Pence: 1 2 5 10 20 50

4 Which coin is worth **less than** 10 pence?

A   B   C   D

5 Which is not a real coin or note?

A   B   C  D

Think!

How many ways can you make 50 pence using

 , and ?

You can use each coin more than once.

These words might help you.

pence   coin

five   ten   two

is equal to

Pounds: 1 2 5 10 20 50   133

Unit 16
Time

In this unit we will …
- ⚡ Say if things happen before or after one another
- ⚡ Use a calendar
- ⚡ Tell time to the hour and the half hour
- ⚡ Solve time word problems

This is a calendar. Can you use it to find how many days are in a week?

March

Sunday	Monday	Tuesday	Wednesday	Thursday	Friday	Saturday
			1	2	3	4
5	6	7	8	9	10	11
12	13	14	15	16	17	18
19	20	21	22	23	24	25
26	27	28	29	30	31	

We will need some maths words. You may know some of these.

before   after   yesterday

today   tomorrow   day   week

month   year   calendar

hour   minute hand

hour hand   o'clock   half past

There are lots of different types of clock. Do all of these clocks show the same time?

Before and after

Discover

1 **a)** Tell the story.

What things does Nina do **before** school?

b) What things does Nina do **after** school?

Share

I thought about the things that I do before and after school.

a) Before school …

… Nina wakes up …

… She gets dressed …

… She eats her breakfast …

… She brushes her teeth …

… She walks to school …

b) After school …

… Nina says goodbye to her friend …

… She rides her bicycle …

… She reads a book …

Think together

1 Point to what happens **before** and **after** Joe plays football.

2 Say what might happen **before** and **after**.

1. Before   2.   3. After

3 These are five events from a story.

CHALLENGE

Put the events in order.

Then write or tell the story with a partner.

Use words like first, then, next, before and after.

I am going to try to use all 5 words in my story.

139

→ Practice book 1C p97

Days of the week

Discover

Tues

1 **a)** What **day** of the **week** do you think it is?

  b) What day was it **yesterday**?

  What day will it be **tomorrow**?

Share

a)

I could see that the teacher was going to write Tuesday.

Yesterday is the day before today.
Tomorrow is the day after today.

b)

Monday
Tuesday
Wednesday
Thursday
Friday
Saturday
Sunday

Yesterday must have been Monday. This is the day before Tuesday.

Tomorrow must be Wednesday. This is the day after Tuesday.

I practised saying the days of the week with a partner.

Think together

1 Which day comes next?

a)

Monday	Tuesday	Wednesday	

b)

Thursday	Friday	Saturday	

c)

Friday	Saturday	Sunday	

2 Today is Thursday.

Monday	Tuesday	Wednesday	Thursday	Friday

a) What is Jacob doing today?
b) What did Jacob do yesterday?
c) What is Jacob going to do tomorrow?

3 Sunday

Monday

Tuesday

Wednesday

Thursday

Friday

Saturday

I can use yesterday, today and tomorrow to talk about the weather.

a) What was the weather like before Tuesday?

b) What was the weather like on the day after Wednesday?

143

→ Practice book 1C p100

Months of the year

Discover

Meg

This is my birthday!

1 **a)** When is Meg's birthday?

b) Use a **calendar** to work out how many **months** there are in a **year**.

Share

a) The calendar shows Meg's birthday is in the month of November.

The square marked has the number 19 in it.

Her birthday is on Sunday 19 November.

November

S	M	T	W	T	F	S
			1	2	3	4
5	6	7	8	9	10	11
12	13	14	15	16	17	18
19	20	21	22	23	24	25
26	27	28	29	30		

b) A calendar shows there are 12 months in a year.

A calendar shows you how many days are in each month.

January

S	M	T	W	T	F	S
1	2	3	4	5	6	7
8	9	10	11	12	13	14
15	16	17	18	19	20	21
22	23	24	25	26	27	28
29	30	31				

February

S	M	T	W	T	F	S
			1	2	3	4
5	6	7	8	9	10	11
12	13	14	15	16	17	18
19	20	21	22	23	24	25
26	27	28				

March

S	M	T	W	T	F	S
			1	2	3	4
5	6	7	8	9	10	11
12	13	14	15	16	17	18
19	20	21	22	23	24	25
26	27	28	29	30	31	

April

S	M	T	W	T	F	S
						1
2	3	4	5	6	7	8
9	10	11	12	13	14	15
16	17	18	19	20	21	22
23	24	25	26	27	28	29
30						

May

S	M	T	W	T	F	S
	1	2	3	4	5	6
7	8	9	10	11	12	13
14	15	16	17	18	19	20
21	22	23	24	25	26	27
28	29	30	31			

June

S	M	T	W	T	F	S
				1	2	3
4	5	6	7	8	9	10
11	12	13	14	15	16	17
18	19	20	21	22	23	24
25	26	27	28	29	30	

July

S	M	T	W	T	F	S
						1
2	3	4	5	6	7	8
9	10	11	12	13	14	15
16	17	18	19	20	21	22
23	24	25	26	27	28	29
30	31					

August

S	M	T	W	T	F	S
		1	2	3	4	5
6	7	8	9	10	11	12
13	14	15	16	17	18	19
20	21	22	23	24	25	26
27	28	29	30	31		

September

S	M	T	W	T	F	S
					1	2
3	4	5	6	7	8	9
10	11	12	13	14	15	16
17	18	19	20	21	22	23
24	25	26	27	28	29	30

October

S	M	T	W	T	F	S
1	2	3	4	5	6	7
8	9	10	11	12	13	14
15	16	17	18	19	20	21
22	23	24	25	26	27	28
29	30	31				

November

S	M	T	W	T	F	S
			1	2	3	4
5	6	7	8	9	10	11
12	13	14	15	16	17	18
19	20	21	22	23	24	25
26	27	28	29	30		

December

S	M	T	W	T	F	S
					1	2
3	4	5	6	7	8	9
10	11	12	13	14	15	16
17	18	19	20	21	22	23
24	25	26	27	28	29	30
31						

Think together

1 When is Charlie's birthday?

Think about the month, the number of the day in the month and the day of the week.

2

I am going horse riding on 8 July.

Point to the day when Izzy is going horse riding.

3

a) How many months are in the year?

b) What are the months?

c) Which months have 30 days?

d) Can you find your birthday?

→ Practice book 1C p103

Tell the time to the hour

Discover

1 **a)** What time does the clock say?

b) The party starts at 5 **o'clock**.

What will the clock show?

Share

a)

There are two hands on a clock. I saw that there was a difference between them.

The longer hand is the **minute hand**. When it points to 12, it shows an o'clock time.

The shorter hand is the **hour hand**. This tells us the **hour** that it is.

The clock says that the time is 3 o'clock.

I now know how to draw other o'clock times.

b) The hour hand will point to 5 and the minute hand will point to 12.

I think there is one hour between o'clock times.

Think together

1 What time is it?

The time is ☐ o'clock.

2 What time is it?

The time is ☐ o'clock.

3 What mistake has each child made?

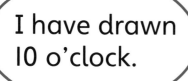

I have drawn 10 o'clock.

I have drawn 4 o'clock.

Harry

Maya

Draw or make the times they should have made.

→ Practice book 1C p106

Tell the time to the half hour

Discover

1 **a)** What time is it now?

b) What will the clock look like when it is time for assembly?

Share

a) The minute hand is half-way around the clock. It is pointing to the number 6.

When the minute hand points to 6, it shows a half-past time.

At **half-past** times, always look at the number that the hour hand has moved half-way past.

The hour hand is half-way between the 9 and 10. I think that means the time is half-way between 9 o'clock and 10 o'clock.

The time is half past 9.

b) Assembly is at half past 10.

The clock will look like this:

I used my finger to trace the clock hands at half past 10.

153

Think together

1 What time is it?

The time is half past ☐.

2 What time is it?

The time is half past ☐.

3

CHALLENGE

I have drawn half past 8.

I have drawn half past 2.

Myra

Filip

What mistake has each child made?

I am going to draw what each clock should look like.

→ Practice book 1C p109

End of unit check

Your teacher will ask you these questions.

1 Which month comes after March?

A February C April

B May D June

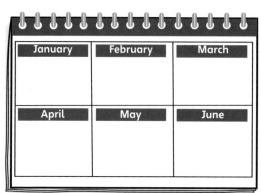

January February March

April May June

2 Harry's birthday is on 25 July.

What day of the week is Harry's birthday?

A Tuesday C Thursday

B Friday D Saturday

July

S	M	T	W	T	F	S
						1
2	3	4	5	6	7	8
9	10	11	12	13	14	15
16	17	18	19	20	21	22
23	24	25	26	27	28	29
30	31					

3 Which clock is showing 9 o'clock?

A  B  C  D

4 Harry goes to bed at this time.
Mia goes to bed 2 hours later.
What time does Mia go to bed?

A half past 7   **C** half past 9

B 9 o'clock   **D** half past 5

5 Anya is going on holiday
on 15 August for 7 days.

When will she
come home?

July						
S	M	T	W	T	F	S
						1
2	3	4	5	6	7	8
9	10	11	12	13	14	15
16	17	18	19	20	21	22
23	24	25	26	27	28	29
30	31					

Think!

Look at these two clocks.
What's the same? What's different?

These words
might help you.

minute hand

hour hand

half past

157

→ **Practice book 1C p112**

I am proud of how much we have learnt this year.

What we have learnt

Can you do all these things?

⚡ Count in 10s, 5s and 2s

⚡ Make arrays

⚡ Find halves and quarters

⚡ Describe position and direction

⚡ Work with numbers up to 100

⚡ Count with coins and notes

⚡ Use a calendar and start to tell the time

Now you are ready to continue your maths journey in Year 2!

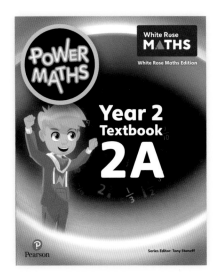

Published by Pearson Education Limited, 80 Strand, London, WC2R 0RL.

www.pearsonschools.co.uk

Text © Pearson Education Limited 2017, 2023
Edited by Pearson and Florence Production Ltd
First edition edited by Pearson, Little Grey Cells Publishing Services and Haremi Ltd
Designed and typeset by Pearson and PDQ Digital Media Solutions Ltd
First edition designed and typeset by Kamae Design
Original illustrations © Pearson Education Limited 2017, 2023
Illustrated by Fran and David Brylewski, Nigel Dobbyn, Adam Linley, Nadene Naude and Jorge Santillan at
Beehive Illustration; Emily Skinner at Graham-Cameron Illustration; Paul Higgins at Hunter-Higgins Design;
and Kamae Design
Images: The Royal Mint, 1971, 1982, 1990, 1992, 1997, 1998, 2017: 118–133; Bank of England: 121, 123–127, 129,
131–133
Cover design by Pearson Education Ltd
Front and back cover illustrations by Will Overton at Advocate Art and Nadene Naude at Beehive Illustration.

Series Editor: Tony Staneff
Lead author: Josh Lury
Consultant (first edition): Professor Liu Jian and Professor Zhang Dan

The rights of Tony Staneff and Josh Lury to be identified as authors of this work have been asserted by them in
accordance with the Copyright, Designs and Patents Act 1988.

First published 2017
This edition first published 2023

24
10 9 8 7 6 5 4 3

British Library Cataloguing in Publication Data
A catalogue record for this book is available from the British Library

ISBN 978 1 292 41969 5

Printed in the UK by Bell & Bain Ltd, Glasgow

For Power Maths resources go to
www.activelearnprimary.co.uk

Note from the publisher
Pearson has robust editorial processes, including answer and fact checks, to ensure the accuracy of the content in this
publication, and every effort is made to ensure this publication is free of errors. We are, however, only human, and
occasionally errors do occur. Pearson is not liable for any misunderstandings that arise as a result of errors in this
publication, but it is our priority to ensure that the content is accurate. If you spot an error, please do contact us at
resourcescorrections@pearson.com so we can make sure it is corrected.